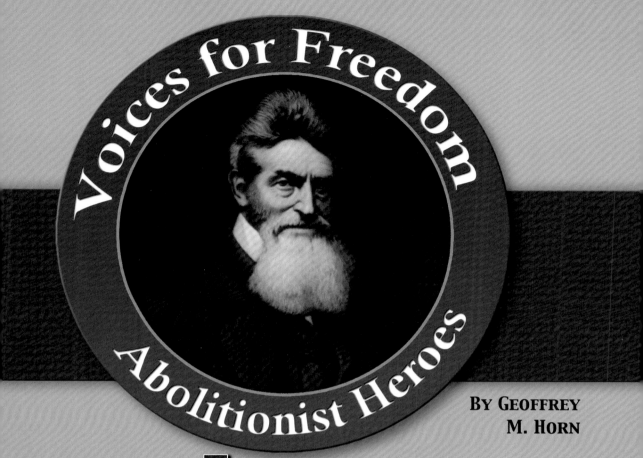

Voices for Freedom
Abolitionist Heroes

By Geoffrey M. Horn

John Brown

Putting Actions Above Words

CRABTREE
Publishing Company
www.crabtreebooks.com

Author: Geoffrey Michael Horn
Publishing plan research and development:
  Sean Charlebois, Reagan Miller
  Crabtree Publishing Company
Editors: Mark Sachner, Lynn Peppas
Proofreader: Ellen Rodger
Editorial director: Kathy Middleton
Photo research: Ruth Owen
Designer: Westgrapix/Tammy West
Production coordinator: Margaret Amy Salter
Production: Kim Richardson
Curriculum adviser: Suzy Gazlay, M.A.
Editorial consultant: James Marten, Ph.D.; Chair, Department
  of History, Marquette University, Milwaukee, Wisconsin

Front cover (inset), back cover, and title page: Photograph of
John Brown.
Front cover (bottom): A series of anti-slavery trading cards from the
1800s, by American artist Henry Louis Stephens. Pictures like this
were used by abolitionists to convince people that slavery should
be stopped.

Written, developed, and produced by Water Buffalo Books

Publisher's note:
All quotations in this book come from original sources and contain
the spelling and grammatical inconsistencies of the original text. Some
of the quotations may also contain terms that are no longer in use and
may be considered inappropriate or offensive. The use of such terms
is for the sake of preserving the historical and literary accuracy of the
sources and should not be seen as encouraging or endorsing the use
of such terms today.

Photographs and reproductions
Canton Historical Society: page 23. Corbis: page 10 (left); John
Carnemolla: page 22; page 24 (top); page 30; page 57 (top).
Bruce S. Ford, City of Akron, Ohio: page 34 (top). Galen
Frysinger: page 33. Getty Images: page 5 (center); page 7; page
11; page 19 (bottom); page 20; page 24 (bottom); page 29; page
31 (top); Stan Wayman: page 31 (bottom); page 35; page 48.
The Granger Collection: page 6; page 15; page 25; page 36;
page 41 (bottom); page 42; page 43 (bottom); page 44: page 46;
page 47; page 54; page 56. Johnbrown.org: page 41 (top).
Courtesy of the Library of Congress: Image 3a22701: page 1;
page 3; page 4 (top left); poster: page 5 (bottom); Image
3g02525: page 9; Image 3a12743: page 10 (right); Image
3a22701: page 15 (top left); Image 07842: page 17; Image
3a22701: page 25 (top left); Image 3a22701: page 32 (top left);
Image 3c06337: page 32; Image 3b48540: page 37; Image 02633:
page 38 (top); Image 3g04550: page 39; Image 3a22701: page 32
(top left); Image 3b26377: page 45; Image 07773: page 49
(bottom); Image 3a22701: page 52 (top left); Image 3a53020:
page 52 (center); Image 3b24611: page 53 (top); Image 3c32541:
page 53 (center); Image 3c32551: page 57 (bottom). North
Wind Archives: page 4; page 12; page 16; page 27; page 28.
Joyce Ranieri: page 58 (left); page 58 (right). Shutterstock: page
5 (top); page 19 (top); page 21; page 51 (top). Superstock: page
8; page 40. Frank Thompson: page 49 (top). West Virginia
Archives and History: page 34 (bottom). Wikipedia (public
domain): page 13; page 14; page 38 (bottom left); page 38
(bottom right); page 51 (bottom); page 60.

Library and Archives Canada Cataloguing in Publication
Horn, Geoffrey M.
  John Brown : putting actions above words / Geoffrey Michael
Horn.

(Voices for freedom: abolitionist heros)
Includes index.
ISBN 978-0-7787-4823-6 (bound).--ISBN 978-0-7787-4839-7 (pbk.)

  1. Brown, John, 1800-1859--Juvenile literature.
2. Abolitionists--United States--Biography--Juvenile literature.
3. Antislavery movements--United States--History--19th
century--Juvenile literature. I. Title. II. Series: Voices for
freedom: abolitionist heros

E451.H67 2009   j973.7'114092   C2009-904187-1 -1

Library of Congress Cataloging-in-Publication Data
Horn, Geoffrey M.
 John Brown : putting actions above words / Geoffrey Michael
Horn.
  p. cm. -- (Voices for freedom: abolitionist heros)
 Includes index.
 ISBN 978-0-7787-4839-7 (pbk. : alk. paper) -- ISBN 978-0-7787-
4823-6 (reinforced library binding : alk. paper)
1. Brown, John, 1800-1859--Juvenile literature. 2. Abolitionists--
United States--Biography--Juvenile literature. 3. Antislavery
movements--United States--History--19th century--Juvenile litera-
ture. I. Title. II. Series.

 E451.H76 2009
 973.7'114--dc22

2009027275

Crabtree Publishing Company

www.crabtreebooks.com   1-800-387-7650

**Published
in Canada
Crabtree Publishing**
616 Welland Ave.
St. Catharines, Ontario
L2M 5V6

**Published in
the United States
Crabtree Publishing**
PMB16A
350 Fifth Ave., Suite 3308
New York, NY 10118

**Published in the
United Kingdom
Crabtree Publishing**
Maritime House
Basin Road North, Hove
BN41 1WR

**Published
in Australia
Crabtree Publishing**
386 Mt. Alexander Rd.
Ascot Vale (Melbourne)
VIC 3032

Contents

CHAPTER ONE

Acts of Blood

O n the night of November 7, 1837, an angry mob gathered outside a warehouse in Alton, Illinois, on the banks of the Mississippi River. Inside the warehouse stood Elijah Parish Lovejoy and 20 of his friends and supporters. Lovejoy, a minister and newspaperman, had seen mobs like this before.

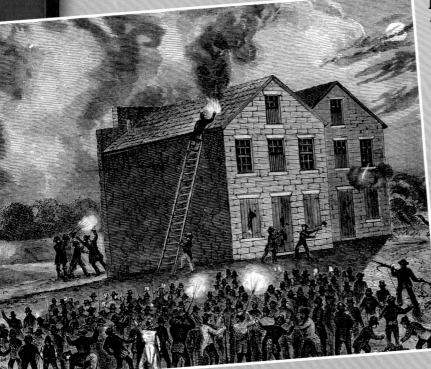

No Stranger to Hatred

At his previous job, across the river in St. Louis, Missouri, Lovejoy had seen a slave, Francis McIntosh, die a horrible death after a mob set him on fire. The experience turned Lovejoy into a fierce opponent of slavery.

The 1837 mob attack on the *Alton Observer*, vividly shown in an engraving from that time.

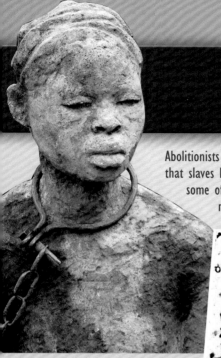

Abolitionists like John Brown and Elijah Lovejoy were outraged by the suffering that slaves had to endure. This powerful portrayal of a woman in chains conveys some of the pain and shame of slavery. The statue is part of a slave memorial on the African island of Zanzibar.

TO BE SOLD, on board the Ship *Bance-Island*, on tuesday the 6th of *May* next, at *Ashley-Ferry*; a choice cargo of about 250 fine healthy NEGROES, just arrived from the Windward & Rice Coast. —The utmost care has already been taken, and shall be continued, to keep them free from the least danger of being infected with the SMALL-POX, no boat having been on board, and all other communication with people from *Charles-Town* prevented.

Austin, Laurens, & Appleby.

N. B. Full one Half of the above Negroes have had the SMALL-POX in their own Country.

The violent conflict over slavery that erupted in the mid-1800s was the climax of a struggle that had been going on for a long time. The advertisement (left), printed in Boston about 1700, offers "a choice cargo of about 250 fine healthy Negroes." The poster (below) calls on opponents of abolition to obstruct an anti-slavery meeting in 1837.

His articles made pro-slavery readers furious. In July 1836, a St. Louis mob smashed his printing press.

Lovejoy moved to Alton in 1837. There he began writing anti-slavery articles for the *Alton Observer*. Three separate times, Alton mobs stormed the warehouse where the *Observer* was printed, stole the printing press, and threw it in the river. At 3:00 a.m. on November 7, a steamboat delivered a fourth printing press, shipped to Alton by the Ohio Anti-Slavery Society. Lovejoy was defending the printing press that night when he was killed by a blast from a rioter's shotgun.

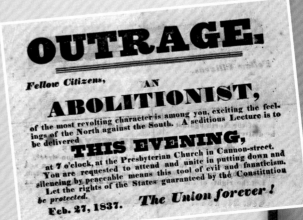

OUTRAGE.

Fellow Citizens, AN ABOLITIONIST, of the most revolting character is among you, exciting the feelings of the North against the South. A seditious Lecture is to be delivered THIS EVENING, at 7 o'clock, at the Presbyterian Church in Cannon-street. You are requested to attend and unite in putting down and silencing by peaceable means this tool of evil and fanaticism. Let the rights of the States guaranteed by the Constitution be protected.

Feb. 27, 1837. *The Union forever!*

Eyewitness to Mob Violence

Elijah Lovejoy died on the night of November 7, 1837, while trying to keep thugs from setting fire to the building where the *Alton Observer* was printed. Here is how Lovejoy's newspaper described the scene after he was killed:

By this time the warehouse roof had begun to burn. The men remaining inside knew they had no choice but to surrender the press.

The mob rushed into the vacant building.

The press Lovejoy died defending was carried to a window and thrown out onto the river bank. It was broken into pieces that were scattered in the Mississippi River.

Fearing more violence, Lovejoy's friends did not remove his body from the building until the next morning.

Members of the crowd from the night before, feeling no shame at what they had done, laughed and jeered as the funeral wagon moved slowly down the street toward Lovejoy's home. Lovejoy was buried on November 9, 1837, his 35th birthday.

This engraving depicts the savagery of the mob that attacked Elijah Lovejoy's printing press, destroyed the building in which it was housed, and murdered Lovejoy.

The View from Hudson, Ohio

News of Lovejoy's death spread quickly. Opponents of slavery were shocked at the fury of the mob. In 1837, most abolitionists hoped that differences over slavery might be settled peacefully. Lovejoy's death was a warning of how violent the conflict over slavery would become.

In few places was the loss of Lovejoy felt more keenly than in Hudson, Ohio. Located in the northeastern part of the state, Hudson was a center of anti-slavery activity and an important stop on the Underground Railroad. The Underground Railroad was a network of people opposed to slavery who helped tens of thousands of African-American slaves escape to freedom. Runaway slaves passed through Hudson on their way to cities farther north, along Lake Erie. From there, the escaped slaves could travel by steamboat to safety in Canada. One of the leaders of the Underground Railroad in Hudson was a white man, John Brown.

Brown had been against slavery his whole life. Like most abolitionists, he was a very religious man who believed the enslavement of black people was "a great sin against God." As a "station master" on the Underground Railroad, he had hidden slaves in his barn. This was risky. The penalty against people caught helping runaway slaves in Ohio was $1,000 per slave.

Slavery had no fiercer opponent than John Brown. This photo of him was taken in the 1850s.

The Underground Railroad helped thousands of slaves escape to freedom. John Brown was active in the Underground Railroad, as were many members of his family.

John Brown's Vow

After Lovejoy's death, John Brown and his father, Owen Brown, attended a memorial service in Hudson. The main speaker was Laurens P. Hickok, a college professor and abolitionist. "The crisis has come," Hickok said. He proposed that Ohio send yet another printing press to Alton and a new person to run it. "If a like fate attends them, send another, till the whole country is aroused," he continued. "And if you can find no fitter man for the first victim, send me."

Many other people spoke. They discussed Hickok's idea and made proposals of their own. As speaker followed speaker, John Brown sat silently, letting the rage boil up inside him. Finally, he could no longer hold back his anger. He stood up, raised his right hand, and said defiantly:

> *Here, before God, in the presence of these witnesses, from this time, I consecrate my life to the destruction of slavery!*

To Brown, these weren't just words. They were a sacred vow.

A Call to Arms

For decades, abolitionists had been talking about slavery. Many abolitionists were pacifists who believed that violence in any form and for any reason was unjustifiable and that all disputes should be settled by peaceful methods. These abolitionists recognized the violence inherent in the institution of slavery. Rather than resort to violent tactics themselves, they hoped to end slavery by persuading slave owners that buying and selling other human beings was wrong.

Brown thought this approach was certain to fail. He believed the slave owners would not give up without a fight.

Brown thought of slavery as a kind of war. The slave owners had used every available weapon to break their slaves in body and spirit. Defenders of slavery would stop at nothing to silence their opponents. The only way to destroy slavery, Brown believed, was for African Americans and their white supporters to take up arms against it.

Brown spent the next 22 years getting ready for battle. By 1839 he had told his wife and oldest children about his plans and asked them to join him. In 1847, he met with African-American abolitionist Frederick Douglass. Brown unfolded a map of the United States, pointed his finger at the Appalachian Mountains, and showed Douglass the area where he thought the war against slavery would begin.

Breaking up slave families was one way that slave owners broke slaves' spirits. "The Parting," created around 1863 by the American artist Henry Louis Stephens, shows a black man in chains sold to a new master, as the slave's wife and child plead to go with him.

THE PARTING "Buy us too."

The question of violence divided the abolitionists. Both Frederick Douglass (left) and William Lloyd Garrison (right) started out believing that the struggle against slavery had to be nonviolent. Later, Douglass supported Brown's plan to wage war against slavery, while Garrison continued to oppose war and bloodshed.

Douglass said he still thought a nonviolent solution might be found. Brown said no. "He knew their proud hearts," Douglass later recalled Brown saying. "They would never be induced to give up their slaves, until they felt a big stick about their heads."

Preparing for War

For a while, Brown continued to rely on nonviolent methods. In 1849, he settled on a farm in North Elba, a rocky region in New York state. There he helped a group of African Americans work the land. North Elba was a stop on the Underground Railroad. As he had in Hudson, Ohio, Brown offered support and shelter to runaway slaves when they reached North Elba.

During the 1850s, Brown focused more sharply on the armed struggle he knew was coming. In 1851, he formed a group in Springfield, Massachusetts, to help slaves arm and defend themselves against slave catchers. In October 1855 he arrived in Kansas, where a bitter and bloody struggle between pro-slavery and anti-slavery settlers was already under way. In May 1856, a group under his command attacked and killed five pro-slavery settlers at Pottawatomie Creek.

Striking a Blow for Freedom

All the while, Brown was plotting the raid for which he would forever be remembered. In order for the war against slavery to succeed, he reasoned, the slaves would need weapons. The United States government stored 100,000 weapons at Harpers Ferry, Virginia, about 65 miles (105 kilometers) from Washington, D.C. In July 1859, Brown rented a Maryland farmhouse within striking distance of the arsenal. There he gathered men and supplies for the attack on Harpers Ferry.

Brown and his tiny army of fewer than two dozen men seized control of the arsenal on October 16. Their success did not last long. Two days later, the arsenal was retaken by federal troops. Ten of Brown's men—including two of his sons—were killed in the fighting.

Brown was arrested and charged with murder and treason. He was convicted by a jury on November 2 and hanged on the gallows a month later. As the date of his death approached, he received a visit in jail from one of his supporters, a Quaker woman named Rebecca Spring. Speaking in a calm voice, he told her:

> *I John Brown am now quite certain that the crimes of this guilty, land: will never be purged away; but with Blood.*

In the decade before the Civil War, pro-slavery and anti-slavery forces clashed in Kansas. This illustration shows pro-slavery forces killing a group of "free soil" settlers in 1858.

In the final hours of his life, he handed this note to one of his guards:

> *I think I cannot now better serve the cause I love so much than to die for it, and in my death I may do more than in my life.*

Fanatic or Freedom Fighter?

In death as in life, opinions about Brown were deeply divided. A leading Southern newspaper called him a "notorious horse thief, murderer, and traitor." Another writer called him "the prince of assassins and thieves." Defenders of slavery described him as extreme, fanatical—even crazy.

Abolitionists took a different view. Frederick Douglass, who had refused to join the Harpers Ferry raid, said in 1881 that Brown could be called "our noblest American hero."

Two of Brown's sons, Watson and Oliver, were killed in the Harpers Ferry raid. This illustration shows Brown with his two dying sons, in the hours before he was captured by federal troops.

"A Great Wrong Against God and Humanity"

After he was captured at Harpers Ferry in October 1859, Brown spoke with his captors about why he had attacked the arsenal. One of his questioners was James Murray Mason, a U.S. senator from Virginia.

Mason: What was your object in coming?
Brown: We came to free the slaves, and only that....
Mason: How do you justify your acts?
Brown: I think, my friend, you are guilty of a great wrong against God and humanity,—I say it without wishing to be offensive,—and it would be perfectly right for any one to interfere with you so far as to free those who you willfully and wickedly hold in bondage. I do not say this insultingly.
Mason: I understand that.
Brown: I think I did right, and that others will do right, who interfere with you at any time and at all times. I hold that the Golden Rule, "Do unto others as ye would that others should do unto you," applies to all who would help others to gain their liberty.

Senator James Murray Mason of Virginia questioned Brown after his capture. Mason, a defender of slavery, was later expelled from the Senate for supporting the Confederacy.

Even those who were not abolitionists paid tribute to the man for his courage and his goals, if not always for the methods he used to accomplish his goals. In anti-slavery churches throughout the North, bells tolled in Brown's honor. On the day of his death, banks, businesses, and government offices closed in Akron, Ohio, to show respect for the man opponents of slavery saw as a great freedom fighter.

Brown could be a difficult man. He held strong religious beliefs and was unbending on matters of principle. He refused to compromise even when the odds were stacked against him.

Brown believed to his dying day that the great evil of slavery would not be ended without blood. History proved him right. The Civil War erupted less than a year and a half after his hanging. In the bloodshed that followed, more than 600,000 Americans died before slavery was outlawed throughout the United States.

Legend has it that on his way to the gallows on December 2, 1859, Brown stopped to kiss an African-American child. The legend is reflected in this painting made by Thomas Hovenden in the 1880s.

CHAPTER TWO

Learning to Hate Slavery

John Brown was born in Torrington, Connecticut, on May 9, 1800. When he arrived, his parents Owen and Ruth Mills Brown, had already been married for seven years. Their first child, Salmon, entered the world in 1794. He died two years later. Their second child died in childbirth around the same time.

Punishment and Forgiveness

The two deaths had a shattering effect on Owen and Ruth. Owen was afraid that God was punishing him because he had not been a good enough Christian. He prayed for forgiveness and believed God had shown mercy to him when Ruth gave birth to a healthy daughter, Anna, in 1798 and then to John. Owen and Ruth also adopted an infant, Levi Blakeslee, soon after they'd married. Ruth gave birth to three more children between 1801 and 1807.

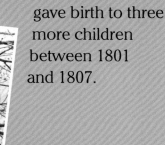

An image of the Connecticut farmhouse where John Brown was born in 1800. The building burned down because of a chimney fire in 1918.

The World of Owen Brown

Thin, hardworking, and God-fearing, Owen Brown spoke with a stammer that bothered him for most of his life. He was a farmer and tanner, skilled at turning animal skins into leather, from which he then made shoes. He was only five years old in 1776 when his father, a captain on the American side in the Revolutionary War, fell ill and died at an army camp near New York City.

Owen's mother, pregnant with her 11th child, had a tough time keeping the family together. A neighbor loaned her a black slave named Sam to help plow the fields. Owen took an immediate liking to Sam, who delighted him by carrying him on his back. When Sam died, his mother brought Owen to the funeral.

Two other events helped shape Owen's ideas about slavery and religion. As a teenager, he found work repairing shoes in the town of West Simsbury, Connecticut. One of the people who hired him was a Congregationalist minister, Jeremiah Hallock, who also taught Owen about God. One day, Owen heard Hallock talking with another minister about slavery, which Hallock described as a sin.

John Brown's grandfather died in 1776 while serving with the Continental Army during the Revolutionary War. American soldiers had to endure harsh conditions that year, including this icy crossing of the Delaware River.

A Pilgrim Ancestor?

In a letter written in 1857, Brown proudly claimed that one of his father's ancestors had come to America on the *Mayflower* in 1620. The man he had in mind was the woodworker Peter Browne. Recent research shows that Peter was born in England in the mid-1590s. He was one of 41 men who signed the Mayflower Compact in November 1620, before the Pilgrim ship landed at Plymouth.

The Mayflower Compact was one of the founding documents of American self-government. In it, the signers pledged to obey the laws and leaders freely chosen by community members.

Historians differ on whether Peter Browne was really John Brown's ancestor. Some accept the family story as true. Others believe Brown's father's family came from another man named Peter Brown, who arrived in Connecticut around 1650.

Pilgrims signing the Mayflower Compact in 1620. The engraved illustration is based on a painting by T. H. Matteson.

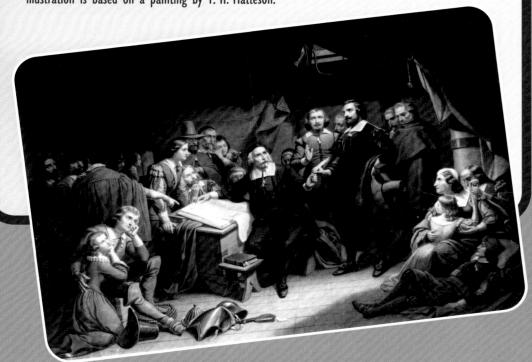

Hallock was pleased that Connecticut had begun to phase out slavery in 1784. Hallock also showed Owen a sermon by a well-known preacher, Jonathan Edwards, Jr. In the sermon, Edwards attacked both slavery and the slave trade.

A second event that had a powerful effect on Owen was a dispute over slavery that took place in the late 1790s. Years earlier, during the Revolutionary War, a minister from the South had traveled to Norfolk, Connecticut, with a family of slaves that he owned. Later, the minister had returned to the South but had left the slave family in Norfolk. When the man came back to Norfolk to reclaim his property, the slaves refused to go with him. At a public hearing in a Norfolk meeting house, the minister defended slavery with arguments that Owen found disgusting. "Ever since, I have been an abolitionist," he said later.

Crime and Punishment

John Brown's mother, Ruth Mills Brown, was the daughter of a minister. A deeply religious young woman, she sang hymns in a clear, sweet voice. "If I have been respected in the world," Owen said, "I must ascribe it more to her than to any other person."

As parents, Ruth and Owen were loving but strict. One of John's earliest memories concerned a mistake he made when he was no more than four years old. He stole three brass pins from a girl who lived with the family. When Ruth found out about it, she did not punish him right away. Instead, she let him feel guilty and fearful for a whole day. Then she gave him a "thorough whipping."

Fear of his parents' discipline led John into a "very *bad & foolish* habit." He began telling lies in order to "screen himself" from blame or punishment. Late in life, he admitted that he had been "often guilty of this fault" and that it had taken him a long time to break the habit.

A Boy on the Frontier

John's father had a tannery in Torrington. The business did not go well. Seeking a fresh start in 1804, Owen scouted out some land in Hudson, Ohio.

The Expansion of Slavery

Abolitionists worked tirelessly to oppose slavery and the slave trade during the first half of the 1800s. Despite their efforts, the total number of African-American slaves continued to grow.

In 1800, the year John Brown was born, the United States had about 894,000 African-American slaves. Three states—Virginia, North Carolina, and Maryland—accounted for about two-thirds of the total. The slave population in the North was much smaller. Brown's home state of Connecticut had begun the process of ending slavery in 1784, when there were several thousand slaves in the state. By 1800, Connecticut had about 950 slaves. That number dropped to 25 by 1830. The state did not completely abolish slavery until 1848.

A ripe cotton plant ready for harvesting.

By 1850, slavery had ended just about everywhere in the North. Meanwhile, the rise of cotton growing in the South greatly increased the demand for slave labor. In two important cotton states—Alabama and Mississippi—the number of slaves rose from about 80,000 in 1820 to more than 650,000 in 1850.

In 1860, on the eve of the Civil War, a census in the United States counted more than 4.4 million African Americans. Almost 90 percent of them were slaves. Free blacks made up a smaller share of the African-American population in 1860 than they had 50 years earlier.

The expansion of slavery in the South during the first half of the 1800s stemmed from a rapid increase in cotton growing.

TANNING.

In the early 1800s, tanning was a foul-smelling process that turned animal skins into leather for clothes and shoes. The hides had to be painstakingly cleaned, soaked, rubbed, and dried.

Hudson was located in a frontier region called the Western Reserve. (Much later, John would remember it as "a wilderness filled with wild beasts, & Indians.") This land had originally been claimed by Connecticut, and a small number of settlers from New England had built homes there.

The Brown family moved to Hudson in 1805. For five-year-old John, the journey by ox-drawn wagon was one of the great adventures of his life. Traveling westward in June and July he "met with Rattle Snakes which were very large; & which some of the company generally managed to kill." He was allowed to ride the horses and help drive the oxen.

Owen and Ruth taught their children to show respect to people of all races. John recalled being "rather afraid of the Indians, & of their Rifles, but this soon wore off." He began to "hang about them" and to learn a little of their languages. At the same time, his father showed him the tanning trade, and he learned how to handle deer, squirrel, cat, dog, wolf, and raccoon skins. He enjoyed running, jumping, and wrestling. Writing of himself in 1857, he said he "was never *quarrelsome*; but was *excessively* fond of the *hardest & roughest* kind of plays."

Love and Loss

For all his love of adventure and rough play, John was a very sensitive boy. As a grown man about to risk his life in a war against slavery, he still was ashamed of a time 50 years earlier when he lost a yellow marble a Native American boy had given him. "It took years to heal the wound," he wrote. On another occasion, young John caught a squirrel that had given him a bad bite. He managed to tame it. When the squirrel ran away or was killed, John mourned the loss "for a year or two." Another source of grief was the death of a lamb he had received as a present, perhaps from his father.

The bitterest blow came when he was eight years old. In December 1808, his mother gave birth for the eighth time. The baby girl died right away, and Ruth passed away a few hours later. John took the loss very hard. A year later, Owen married a 20-year-old woman, Sallie Root, to take care of the

John Brown was five years old when his family moved from Connecticut to Ohio. The trip through the wilderness was made in a wagon much like the one shown here. It was one of the most enjoyable periods of John's life.

young family. John later described her as sensible and smart, "*yet he never adopted her in feeling*." He respected his stepmother "but continued to pine after his own Mother for years."

Life Lessons

John was 12 years old when war broke out in 1812 between the United States and Britain. A U.S. military official, General William Hull, was given the job of defending Ohio and Michigan against the British in the War of 1812. Owen Brown got the job of supplying beef and horses to Hull's troops. John helped his father by rounding up cattle and driving them through the wilderness to Hull's men in Michigan. John took an immediate dislike to the soldiers, who were unruly and used foul language. The experience soured him on military service.

On his way home from Michigan after a cattle drive, John for the first time saw the evils of slavery with his own eyes. He stayed at the home of a man who owned a slave boy about John's age. The man heaped praise on his white guest, complimenting

Cattle drives like this one supplied General William Hull's men with beef on the hoof during the War of 1812.

The Education of John Brown

As a boy, John Brown had little interest in schooling. He much preferred exploring the wilderness or helping his father at the tannery to sitting in the classroom. He disliked math but enjoyed reading history and the Bible.

At the age of 16, he decided he wanted to study to become a minister. Joined by a family friend and one of his younger brothers, he rode on horseback from Hudson, Ohio, to Connecticut. At the urging of his father's old teacher, the minister Jeremiah Hallock, he first enrolled at a Massachusetts school that was run by one of Hallock's relatives. A few months later, he transferred to the Morris Academy in Litchfield, Connecticut. Officials at both schools remembered him as a serious young man and a good student.

Brown's career as a college student ended within a year. Money ran short, and an eye problem interfered with his studies. By the summer of 1817, he was back home in Hudson.

Jeremiah Hallock, an anti-slavery minister, aided the education of both Owen and John Brown.

everything John did and said. The owner's attitude toward his black slave was completely different. John saw right away how poorly the slave was fed, clothed, and housed. Then he watched in horror as the owner beat his slave with an iron shovel.

The brutal treatment of the "Fatherless & Motherless" slave boy by his owner left a lasting impression on John. He described the event as a major step on his path to declaring "*Eternal war* with Slavery."

Witnessing a slave owner's cruelty to a slave boy was a turning point in John Brown's life. It was not unusual for a grown slave's back (above) to show the scars of many whippings. Suspended in the air, with his hands and feet bound, the slave shown in the illustration (right) was powerless to resist an overseer's brutal beating.

CHAPTER THREE

Family Man

B y the time John Brown was 18 years old, he stood about five feet, ten inches (178 centimeters) tall. Lean and well-groomed, he kept his black hair combed straight back. His blue-gray eyes were intense, and he showed little interest in pastimes such as dancing, card playing, or light conversation. Toward people who worked for him, he often seemed arrogant. He "doted on being the head of the heap," said a former classmate, Milton Lusk.

This portrait of Brown was made in 1857. Do you find his expression unsettling? Opponents often used this image of Brown when they wanted to portray him as a madman rather than a freedom fighter.

Making a Mark

In his late teens, Brown and his adopted brother, Levi Blakeslee, set up their own tannery and moved into a log house nearby. Not long after, John and Levi put their anti-slavery beliefs into practice by sheltering a runaway slave. By this time, Owen Brown was already active in Hudson's Underground Railroad. John was eager to make his own mark in the struggle for racial equality.

A "Remarkably Plain" Girl

Brown's work at the tannery kept him extremely busy. To help with cooking and cleaning, he hired Milton Lusk's widowed mother. She accepted the job and moved in along with her daughter Dianthe. There was nothing fancy about the 19-year-old Dianthe. In fact, she impressed Brown as "remarkably plain." He later described her as a "neat industrious & economical girl; of excellent character; earnest piety; & good practical common sense." Brown, often shy around women, asked advice from his father, who urged his son to marry her. Then he asked Dianthe, who said yes, and they were married on June 21, 1820.

One sour note at their wedding was the absence of her brother Milton. Dianthe and Milton had been very close. Before John and Dianthe were married, Milton had come to Brown's home on a Sunday to visit his mother and sister. Brown took an unbending view of the Sabbath. He saw Sunday as the Lord's day, fit for serious prayer and study, not cheery family visits. Sternly, he told Milton to visit on some day other than Sunday. Milton was angry. "John," he said, "I won't come Sunday, nor any other day." Later, when John and Dianthe had children, he refused to let them play or entertain visitors on the Sabbath.

Dianthe gave birth to seven children between 1821 and 1832; five of them lived to become adults. The strain of constant childbearing took a toll on Dianthe's physical and emotional health. Both John and Dianthe were sick for much of 1831, the same year their four-year-old son Frederick died.

When Dianthe became pregnant again, her condition declined still further. The son she delivered on August 7, 1832, was dead at birth, and Dianthe died three days later.

A New Day

Like the loss of his mother in childbirth 24 years earlier, Dianthe's death took its toll on Brown. He felt tired, lonely, and deeply depressed. "I have been pretty much confined to my house for a number of weeks," he wrote. "I feel I am getting more & more unfit for every thing…. I have been growing numb for a good while." Burdened with the task of raising five children, he once again hired a housekeeper, the daughter of a blacksmith, Charles Day.

On more than one occasion, the housekeeper brought along her younger sister, Mary Ann Day, to help spin thread. Mary Ann was 16 years old, sturdy and strong, quiet, and well skilled at the spinning wheel. Brown barely spoke with her. Instead, he wrote a letter asking her to marry him. After some hesitation, she agreed, and their wedding took place on June 14, 1833. While they were married, she gave birth to 13 children, of whom six lived to adulthood.

During John Brown's lifetime, childbirth was risky to mother and baby alike. Births took place at home, with little of the medical knowledge and equipment that are common today. In this illustration, a midwife shows a new baby to a grieving husband whose wife has died while giving birth.

Brown expected his wife and children to obey him without complaint. For the most part, they did. His oldest son, John Brown, Jr., born in 1821, wrote: "Father had a rule not to threaten one of his children. He commanded, and there was obedience."

Business Ups and Downs

Brown constantly needed money to support his expanding family. While living in Hudson, Ohio, in the early 1820s, he had learned of a fantastic business opportunity in northwestern Pennsylvania. In 1825, he bought 200 acres (81 hectares) of good timberland in Pennsylvania's Randolph Township, at the low price of 75 cents an acre. He cleared 25 acres (10 ha) of timber and constructed a log house and a barn with a secret room to shelter runaway slaves.

By the end of the 1820s, he had built a thriving tanning business. In a town he called New Richmond, he started a post office and a school. He was the leader of a new and growing community. Then his luck changed. The economy slowed. His wife Dianthe's death caused him to neglect his

John Brown's second wife, Mary Day Brown (center), is shown with two of their daughters, Annie (left) and Sarah (right), in a photo taken around 1851. Brown expected other members of his family to obey him without question.

Dividing the Chores

Visitors to the Brown household were struck by how equally the chores were divided. All the children were expected to help, both outdoors and indoors. "The mothers, daughters and sons did the serving, and did it well," said Frederick Douglass. "Supper over, the boys helped to clear the table and wash the dishes." Kitchen skills were a point of pride for Brown's sons. Salmon Brown, born in 1836, recalled that the "boys could turn a steak or brown a loaf as well as their mother."

work. By the middle of the decade he was frantic for cash. He left Pennsylvania and returned to Ohio, setting up a tannery in the town of Franklin Mills.

As his debts mounted, Brown looked for a way to break clear. He knew of a plan to build a canal in Ohio. A new canal, Brown thought, was sure to bring trade, jobs, and wealth to the towns along the proposed route, including Franklin Mills. He persuaded family members and friends to lend him more money. With these funds, he bought land near the canal route, expecting to sell the land at a big profit.

His hopes collapsed in the Panic of 1837. The panic was one of the steepest economic downturns in the nation's history. Money became scarce. Banks failed. Businesses shut their doors. The canal company changed its plans. Land that Brown thought might make his fortune turned out to be worthless.

Completion of the Erie Canal in 1825 brought great wealth to New York state. Brown thought a planned new canal might do the same thing for Ohio. He suffered a terrible financial loss when the plan fell through.

The Panic of 1837 left many people with long lists of debts and little money to pay them.

Hitting Bottom

Brown tried desperately to keep his finances afloat. He moved his family back to Hudson. He returned to the tanning trade, and several of his children dropped out of school to assist him. He bought and sold cattle. He tried breeding sheep and selling wool. Nothing helped.

In September 1842, he went bankrupt. He lost almost everything. His family was left with a few household items and some farm animals. He got to keep his collection of 11 Bibles and other religious texts.

As bad as 1842 was for the Brown family, 1843 was worse. Dysentery, an intestinal disease, rampaged through the household. In two short weeks in September, the sickness claimed the lives of four of his children. Brown had hit bottom. He felt, he later said, "a steady, strong, desire; to die."

Standing Up for Equality

A church attended by John Brown and his family placed whites and blacks in separate sections. Whites sat in the best seats in the front. African Americans were expected to sit in the back, where it was harder to see and hear. John's daughter, Ruth Brown Thompson, who was born in 1829, recalled the day her father decided to challenge the church's disgraceful practice:

When I was six or seven years old, a little incident took place in the church at Franklin, Ohio… Father hired a colored man and his wife to work for him,—he on the farm, and she in the house. They were very respectable people, and we thought a great deal of them. One Sunday the woman went to church, and was seated near the door, or somewhere back. This aroused father's indignation at once. He asked both of them to go the next Sunday; they followed the family in, and he seated them in his pew. The whole congregation were shocked; the minister looked angry; but I remember father's firm, determined look…. My brothers were so disgusted to see such a mockery of religion that they left the church, and have never belonged to another.

Throughout Brown's lifetime, and for many years after, blacks were seated separately from whites in many churches, streetcars, and other public places. The illustration (above) shows a black preacher addressing a racially mixed congregation—an uncommon event in South Carolina in 1860. The photo (below) depicts African Americans sitting in the back of a bus in 1956, as required by Florida law at that time.

CHAPTER FOUR

Planning for War

Even as Brown fought unsuccessfully to avoid financial ruin, another conflict was gnawing at him. The battle against slavery was heating up. In a few places, slaves had begun to revolt against their masters.

In Need of a Plan

For a long time, Brown had been helping African Americans escape slavery through the Underground Railroad. He had prodded his neighbors to treat black people more fairly. Had he done enough to combat slavery? Brown felt certain the answer was no.

In 1837, Elijah Lovejoy, a white abolitionist and newspaperman, had given up his life while defending the cause of freedom. Lovejoy's death at the hands of an angry white mob made a deep impression on Brown. If white slave owners were going to fight to keep slavery, African Americans and their

From 1837 onward, Brown was haunted by the need to strike a decisive blow against slavery.

The National Underground Railroad Freedom Center in Cincinnati, Ohio, celebrates the accomplishments of all those, including Brown, who helped fugitive slaves escape to freedom. In this museum display, a candle in the window indicates a house where runaway slaves could find shelter.

abolitionist friends would need to fight back. Brown began working on a battle plan he hoped would end slavery once and for all.

A Way Forward

As he endured the shame of bankruptcy in 1842, followed by the loss of four of his children in 1843, Brown had little time to work on his battle plan.

This impressive stone mansion, completed by Simon Perkins in 1837, still stands today in Akron, Ohio.

That changed after a businessman named Simon Perkins decided to back Brown in the wool trade. Perkins's father—also named Simon—had been one of the founders of Akron, Ohio, and the son ranked among the town's leading citizens. In January 1844, Perkins and Brown signed a contract. The two men agreed to combine their herds of sheep. Brown's job was to tend all the sheep on Perkins's land and then market the wool. Brown was "a rough herdsman, but a nice judge of wool," Perkins said.

Brown moved his family into a house in Akron that Perkins rented to him for $30 a year. Brown was thrilled with the deal. "I think this is the most comfortable and the most favourable arrangement of my worldly concerns that I ever had," he wrote. He was confident the new job would

give him "more leisure for improvement, by day, & by Night…. Our time will all be at our own command except the care of the flock."

In 1846, Brown and his two oldest sons, John Jr. and Jason, set up a wool

Perkins rented this Akron house to Brown and his family in the 1840s, while he and Brown were business partners.

Death of Capt. Ferrer, the Captain of the Amistad, July, 1839.

Don Jose Ruiz and Don Pedro Montez, of the Island of Cuba, having purchased fifty-three slaves at Havana, recently imported from Africa, put them on board the Amistad, Capt. Ferrer, in order to transport them to Principe, another port on the Island of Cuba. After being out from Havana about four days, the African captives on board, in order to obtain their freedom, and return to Africa, armed themselves with cane knives, and rose upon the captain and crew of the vessel. Capt. Ferrer and the cook of the vessel were killed; two of the crew escaped; Ruiz and Montez were made prisoners.

An 1840 engraving depicts the uprising in which a group of slaves (who had been illegally captured) killed the captain of the *Amistad* and took control of the ship. Abolitionists supported the court case through which the slaves eventually gained their freedom.

Slave Revolts

Two events in the 1830s shocked Americans and showed slaves actively resisting the institution that held them in bondage. In August 1831, a slave named Nat Turner led a rebellion in Virginia. He and more than 40 of his followers killed at least 55 white people. Turner was captured in late October and, after a quick trial, was hanged to death on November 11.

Another slave revolt had a happier outcome. In early 1839, slave hunters captured a large group of Africans and illegally shipped them from Africa to Cuba. There, in June, 53 of the slaves were bought by two Spanish planters and put on board the sailing ship *Amistad*. Led by a man named Cinque, the slaves killed the captain of the Amistad and took over the ship. In August, as they sailed north and east along the United States coastline, they were overtaken by U.S. forces and put in jail. A long court battle followed, in which abolitionists aided Cinque and the other slaves. They won their freedom in 1841, and 35 survivors of the original *Amistad* voyage returned home to Africa.

Brown greatly respected both Turner and Cinque. He particularly admired Cinque because his rebellion had resulted in much less bloodshed.

Henry Highland Garnet, an African-American minister and former slave, openly called for slaves to revolt against their masters.

warehouse and marketing center in Springfield, Massachusetts. The following year, he moved his whole family to Springfield. Money that might have been used to furnish their new home was instead sent to help runaway slaves in New York state. When Frederick Douglass visited the Brown household he found "no sofas, no cushions, no curtains, no carpets, no easy rocking chairs. …" Meals of "potatoes and cabbage, and beef soup" were served on a plain pine table.

Meeting with Douglass

Douglass's visit had a serious purpose. Brown had begun meeting with abolitionists and free blacks in Springfield. While traveling in New York, Brown was introduced to a fiery black preacher, Henry Highland Garnet. Garnet was a former slave who, like Brown, believed the time was ripe for rebellion. At a meeting in 1843 of the National Negro Convention in Buffalo, New York, Garnet had said: "Brethren, arise, arise! Strike for your lives and liberties. Now is the day and the hour…. Rather die freemen than live to be slaves."

Garnet told Douglass about the unusual white man in Springfield who seemed to hate slavery as much as many blacks did. Douglass did not share Garnet's views about the need for an immediate uprising. At this time he still hoped to find a nonviolent way to end slavery. Nevertheless, he accepted Brown's invitation to come to Springfield in November 1847.

After dinner, Brown discussed his plan with Douglass. He would begin, said Brown, with a small group of well-armed men. They would set up hideouts in the Appalachian Mountains, where they could easily evade their pursuers. "God has given the strength of the hills to freedom," he told Douglass.

From their mountain strongholds, bands of raiders would attack slave plantations in the South and liberate as many slaves as they could. Freed slaves would be offered guns and invited to join the fight. Slaves who preferred not to wage war would be helped to flee northward via the Underground Railroad.

Brown and Douglass talked from 8:00 P.M. to 3:00 A.M. Douglass raised serious questions about the plan, and Brown did his best to reassure him. Finally, Douglass said he thought the plan "had much to commend it." Soon after, he wrote that Brown, "though a white gentleman, is in [his] sympathy, a black man, and as deeply interested in our cause, as though his own soul had been pierced with the iron of slavery."

For a brief period after the Civil War, some African Americans who had grown up under slavery held prominent positions in the U.S. government. This illustration, published in the early 1880s, combines scenes of pre-Civil War plantation life with portraits of African-American leaders. At the center is Frederick Douglass.

Gerrit Smith backed the North Elba project and, later, Brown's raid at Harpers Ferry.

The Farm at North Elba

In the late 1840s, Brown was forced to deal with a familiar problem: money. The wool business was not going well. His debts were piling up again. He needed a fresh start—a new mission, he hoped, that would also allow him to carry out God's work by helping his black brothers.

In April 1848, Brown visited a wealthy white man, Gerrit Smith, in Peterboro, New York. Smith was a social reformer, an abolitionist, and a loyal supporter of Frederick Douglass. Smith's holdings included about 120,000 acres (48,560 ha) of land in the Adirondack Mountains, near Lake Placid. Smith had carved up his Adirondack land to create farms for thousands of black families. The project was not going well. Smith knew little about farming, and the African Americans who had accepted the offer of cheap land had no experience dealing with the rocky soil and chilly climate of upstate New York.

Brown moved with his family in 1849 to a farmhouse (left) at North Elba, in the Adirondack region of New York state. Inside the farmhouse (right) is a reconstruction of the Browns' plainly furnished parlor. The John Brown Farm and Gravesite, near Lake Placid, is now a National Historic Landmark.

Brown offered to come live on one of the farms, show the black settlers how to work the land, "look after them in all needful ways, and be a kind of father to them." Smith sold him 244 acres (99 ha) of land at North Elba for only $1 an acre, and Brown moved his family there in 1849. For the next several years, he divided his time between North Elba and his wool business in Springfield. He much preferred North Elba, with its magnificent mountain views.

Brown believed that black people and white people should live as equals. At North Elba he often visited his African-American friends in their homes. A white visitor who did not share Brown's views on racial equality noted with surprise that Brown insisted on calling black men "Mister" and inviting them into his home to eat at the same table with his family.

The League of Gileadites

In 1850 the U.S. Congress dealt a terrible blow to opponents of slavery. Yielding to demands by slave owners in the South, Congress passed the Fugitive Slave Act. This unjust law made it a crime for people in the North to help runaway slaves. It also required the federal government to help slave owners get their slaves back. Slaves who were arrested had no right to a fair trial. Instead, their cases were heard by special commissioners. Under the

The Fugitive Slave Act made it much easier for slave catchers to hunt down runaway slaves and return them to slave owners in the South. Passage of this law in 1850 convinced Brown that African Americans needed to arm themselves for their own defense.

Brown based his League of Gileadites on the Bible's account of how Gideon selected his fighting force at Mount Gilead. The French painter from the 1800s, James Jacques Joseph Tissot, depicted this biblical story in "Gideon Chooses the Three Hundred."

law, a commissioner who helped a slave owner reclaim a suspected runaway got $10. The commissioner earned only $5 if the suspect was released.

Brown thought it was time to fight back. In 1851, while in Springfield, he got together a group of more than 40 African Americans. Many were fugitives on the Underground Railroad. He urged them to arm themselves against raids by slave catchers.

Brown called the self-defense group the League of Gileadites. The name referred to Mount Gilead, a place named in the Bible. Mount Gilead played an important part in the story of Gideon, an Israelite leader who had thousands of followers. In the story (as Brown understood it), Gilead was the place where God told Gideon to dismiss most of his followers and keep only the bravest and best fighters. Trusting in the Lord, Gideon and his small army went on to win a great victory.

Members of the League took their mission seriously. When William Wells Brown, an abolitionist and former slave, visited Springfield in 1854, he found black men carrying guns and black women prepared to pour boiling water on any slave catchers who came into their neighborhoods.

A Family Pledge

Late in life, John Brown, Jr., recalled a dramatic moment in 1839 when his father revealed to his pregnant wife Mary and three teenage sons that he was prepared to sacrifice his life in a war to free the slaves. What he needed to know from his family was whether they, too, were ready to dedicate their lives to the same cause.

As John Jr. remembered, his father had been reading the Bible one night when he suddenly looked up and began to speak. "Who among you," Brown asked, "is willing to make common cause with me to break the jaws of the wicked…?"

First he turned to his wife. "Are you, Mary?"

"Yes, husband," she answered.

Next he turned to his oldest son, John Jr. "Are you?" he asked. "Yes, father," John replied. Finally he asked the same question to two of his other sons, Jason and Owen. "Yes, father," each son said. Then they all sank to their knees and prayed together.

When they had finished praying, Brown asked them to raise their right hands and swear an oath. Five decades later, John Jr. could not remember the exact words of the oath they swore that night. "But in substance," he wrote, "it bound us to secrecy and devotion to the purpose of fighting slavery by force and arms to the extent of our ability."

Twenty years after members of John Brown's family made a solemn vow to support his war against slavery, two of his sons died in the raid at Harpers Ferry in 1859. Watson Brown (above) was 24 years old when he was killed, and Oliver (below) was only 20. Another son, Frederick, was 25 years old when he was killed by pro-slavery forces in Kansas in 1856.

He saw the Springfield train station guarded by "some ten or fifteen blacks all armed to the teeth and swearing vengeance upon the heads of any who should attempt to take them."

This was the first time in American history that a white man had organized an army of African Americans to combat slavery. Soon, John Brown would seek to apply the lessons of Gilead to the anti-slavery struggle in Kansas and Harpers Ferry.

The illustration shows Brown meeting with African Americans in Springfield, Massachusetts, after he opened a wool warehouse there in 1846. Later, he helped African Americans in Springfield form a self-defense force, the League of Gileadites.

CHAPTER FIVE

The Road to Harpers Ferry

Seven years before the Civil War broke out in 1861, pro-slavery and anti-slavery forces were already gearing up for battle. Their first major battleground became known as "Bleeding Kansas."

Battle on the Frontier

In 1854, Congress passed the Kansas-Nebraska Act. The law created two new frontier territories, Kansas and Nebraska. In the past, when Congress had established new territories, it had declared which ones would allow slavery and which ones would not. (This policy was known as the Missouri Compromise.) The Kansas-Nebraska Act departed from this practice. Congress did not say in 1854 whether slavery would be permitted or outlawed in the

When Congress created two new territories—Kansas and Nebraska—it sparked a bloody conflict between defenders and opponents of slavery.

43

two new regions. Instead, the law left the decision up to the settlers in each territory.

Nebraska was the more northerly of the two regions. It seemed certain to become a free state. Kansas was another matter. It bordered on Missouri, where slavery was permitted. Slave owners in Missouri feared that Kansas would become a hotbed of abolitionist activity and a haven for runaway slaves. Their fears were well founded.

John Brown Comes to Kansas

Thousands of farmers, ranchers, builders, and traders flooded into Kansas. Some of the newcomers favored slavery; others opposed it. Among the anti-slavery (or "free soil") settlers who arrived in the spring of 1855 were five sons of John Brown. They set up a homestead in southeastern Kansas that was known as Brown's Station.

Tensions rose rapidly between the anti-slavery and pro-slavery groups. In March 1855, some 5,000 pro-slavery "Border Ruffians" crossed into Kansas from Missouri. They elected a pro-slavery legislature.

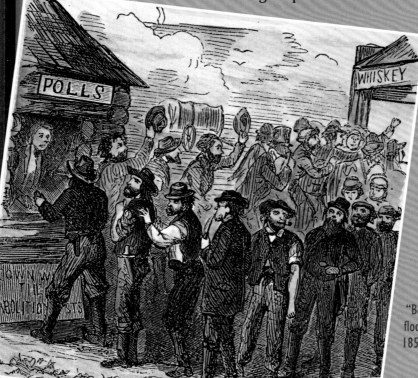

"Border Ruffians" from Missouri flooded into Kickapoo, Kansas, in 1855 to elect a pro-slavery legislature.

The Dred Scott Decision

In 1846, a slave named Dred Scott went to court to seek his freedom. Scott, who was born about 1799, had lived in Virginia, Alabama, and Missouri, where slavery was permitted, and in Illinois and Wisconsin Territory, where slavery was banned. While in Wisconsin, he had married a slave woman, Harriet Robinson. She sued for freedom in 1846 along with her husband.

The case went all the way to the U.S. Supreme Court, which issued its decision in March 1857. Led by Chief Justice Roger B. Taney, a defender of slavery, the Court ruled against Scott and his wife. The decision said that, under the Constitution, slaves were not citizens and never could be. Thus, they had no right to sue for their freedom in federal court. Moreover, the justices said that Congress did not have the power to stop the spread of slavery into federal territories. This ruling further strengthened the provisions of the Kansas-Nebraska Act, which allowed individual territories to decide on their own whether to be free or slave.

The Dred Scott decision made John Brown and other abolitionists very angry. It strengthened Brown's belief that if the courts would not act to end slavery, he would need to take the law into his own hands.

The Dred Scott case was front-page news in 1857. This newspaper displayed portraits of Scott (lower left), his wife Harriet (lower right), and his daughters Eliza and Lizzie (above).

The legislature made it illegal to speak out against slavery. Another law made helping a runaway slave a crime punishable by death.

At first, Brown had not wanted to go to Kansas. His wife, their younger children, and the black settlers of North Elba needed him back in New York state. His mind changed during the summer of 1855, as his sons wrote from Kansas about the threats they faced from illness, foul weather, and the well-armed Border Ruffians. "The storm every day thickens," wrote John Jr. They needed weapons, or money to buy them.

By August 1855, Brown was on his way to Kansas. As he rolled through Ohio, he gave anti-slavery speeches, raised funds and supplies for the Kansas settlers, and visited his ailing father. (The 85-year-old man died the following May.) When Brown, his 16-year-old son Oliver, and his son-in-law Henry Thompson arrived at Brown's Station in October, they were shocked by what they saw. The settlers were weak, ill, and hungry. Brown, who was already in his mid-fifties, set to work with the energy of a man half his age. He nursed the sick, built cabins, and brought in what little remained of the harvest.

Slaughter at Pottawatomie

Life in Kansas was hard, and it was about to get much harder. In early

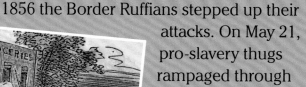

1856 the Border Ruffians stepped up their attacks. On May 21, pro-slavery thugs rampaged through the town of

Lawrence, Kansas, was a hub of "free soil" activity when Border Ruffians ransacked the town in May 1856. The attackers smashed newspaper offices and burned down the Free State Hotel.

Abolitionists reacted with fury at the news that a pro-slavery congressman, Preston S. Brooks of South Carolina, had used his walking stick to bludgeon an anti-slavery senator, Charles Sumner of Massachusetts, in the U.S. Senate chamber. Sumner needed three years to recover from the injuries.

Lawrence, Kansas, which had been a center for anti-slavery activity. A day later, in Washington, D.C., Charles Sumner, a leading anti-slavery senator from Massachusetts, was brutally beaten by a pro-slavery congressman from South Carolina.

When word of these events reached Brown's Station, John Brown demanded revenge. Others urged caution. He would have none of it, saying:

> *Caution … is nothing but the word of cowardice.*

Brown would answer violence with violence, blood with blood. On the night of May 24, he led four of his sons, his son-in-law, and two other men to Pottawatomie Creek.

At Pottawatomie Creek, Brown led a murderous attack on the Doyle family, a group of settlers with pro-slavery sympathies.

Armed with swords and guns, they approached the cabins of settlers they believed were supporters of slavery. They forced five men from their homes and hacked them to death.

Revenge of the Border Ruffians

Some of Brown's men later regretted what they had done. John Brown did not. When his son Jason called the murders a "wicked act," Brown responded,

> *God is my judge. It was absolutely necessary as a measure of self-defence, and for the defence of others.*

Pro-slavery forces answered violence with more violence. After word spread that the Brown clan had carried out the killings, Border Ruffians smashed Brown's Station. Jason and John Jr.—two sons who had not been involved in the Pottawatomie slaughter—were captured and beaten.

The Brown family suffered an even greater loss in a battle later that summer. Border Ruffians attacked the town of Osawatomie on August 30. One of the first to fall was Brown's 25-year-old son Frederick, who was shot through the heart. Brown and a force of about 40 men bravely tried to

The Soldiers' Monument, honoring the defenders of Osawatomie, was dedicated in 1877. John Brown Memorial Park, a National Historic Site, now occupies the area where the battle took place.

defend the town against hundreds of attackers. Greatly outnumbered, Brown's men were forced to retreat. They watched helplessly as the town burned.

Hero or Killer?

When Brown left Kansas in the autumn of 1856, opinions about him were split. To some, he was a murderer and an outlaw. To others, he was a hero. Many abolitionists talked about their hatred of slavery. Brown had actually done something about it.

Brown, who had sheltered so many runaway slaves, was now himself a fugitive. Federal agents were hunting him. Brown hid in the homes of friends and supporters. He traveled under false names like Nelson Hawkins, Shubel Morgan, and Isaac Smith.

Hunted for his role in the Kansas violence, Brown disguised his face with a bushy white beard.

Planning for Rebellion

Brown had not abandoned the plan he had discussed with Frederick Douglass in 1847. Brown's Kansas experience had convinced him that slavery would not be ended without violent rebellion. He continued to prepare for the time when, with God's help, an army of slaves would rise up to overthrow their masters.

Brown believed the freed slaves might form a new state in the Appalachian Mountains. For this new state he wrote a new Constitution. His document was based on the idea of equal rights for African Americans, Native Americans, women, and other groups the original U.S. Constitution had overlooked.

He organized a convention in Chatham, Ontario, a Canadian town that was home to many runaway slaves. After swearing an oath of secrecy, convention members discussed Brown's document. They approved his Constitution and elected him commander-in-chief.

Harpers Ferry and the "Secret Six"

To supply money and weapons for his plan, Brown enlisted a small group of trusted supporters. These abolitionists became known as the "Secret Six." One of the six was Gerrit Smith, whom Brown had worked with at North Elba.

Brown knew where he would strike first: the federal arsenal at Harpers Ferry, near the Blue Ridge Mountains of northern Virginia. The arsenal held about 100,000 rifles and muskets—enough to supply a large army of freed slaves.

In the summer of 1859, Brown again discussed his plan with Douglass, asking him to join the raid on Harpers Ferry. Douglass said no. He pointed out that in raiding the federal arsenal, Brown wasn't just striking a blow at slavery in the South—he was attacking U.S. government property. Douglass warned Brown that he was "going into a perfect steel-trap … and would never get out alive."

Where Is Harpers Ferry?

The U.S. arsenal and nearby town of Harpers Ferry were located near the northern end of the Shenandoah River Valley, where the Shenandoah and Potomac rivers meet. At the time of John Brown's raid, this area belonged to the state of Virginia. During the Civil War, Union and Confederate armies fought hard over Harpers Ferry, and the town changed hands eight times.

Harpers Ferry, in present-day West Virginia, as seen from across the border with Maryland.

While the war raged, Virginia split in two, with the northwestern region supporting the Union and eastern and southern areas backing the Confederacy. The northwestern region entered the Union in 1863 as the state of West Virginia.

After the war, Harpers Ferry became part of West Virginia. Today, it is surrounded by Harpers Ferry National Historical Park. The park covers land in West Virginia as well as parts of Virginia and Maryland.

Originally constructed in 1848 to serve as a guard house and to hold fire engines, this building is known today as "Brown's Fort." Brown and his followers made their last stand here as federal troops retook Harpers Ferry.

CHAPTER SIX

Judging John Brown

The just man shall be in eternal remembrance

Gave his Life for the Liberation of the Slave.

Hero or villain? Success or failure? Historians continue to debate the meaning of John Brown's life and death.

I t all seemed innocent enough. On July 3, 1859, a bearded old man arrived in the town of Harpers Ferry. He called himself Isaac Smith and said he was a cattle buyer from New York state. He said he was looking for a quiet place where he and a few others could spend the rest of the year.

At the Kennedy Farm

A day later—on Independence Day— John Brown crossed the Potomac River into Maryland and began looking for a secluded site from which he hoped to launch his rebellion. He settled on an old farmhouse and cabin that had belonged to Dr. Booth Kennedy. The farm was located about 5 miles (8 km) from the federal arsenal. He paid $35 to rent the farm through the following March—far longer than he would need.

Brown had recruited 21 men for the Harpers Ferry raid. Sixteen of the men were white, and five

Brown and his followers lived at the Kennedy farm (above) from July to mid-October 1859, as they prepared for the Harpers Ferry raid. When their attack plan went sour, the raiders and their hostages took refuge in the engine house (left), the interior of which is depicted here.

were African American. Three of the white people were Brown's sons Owen, Watson, and Oliver. As the men began arriving, some of the neighbors became curious. They thought "Mr. Smith" might be running a station on the Underground Railroad.

To maintain the appearance of normalcy, Brown invited his 15-year-old daughter Annie and Oliver's wife Martha down from North Elba. The young women cooked, cleaned, chatted cheerfully with visitors, and kept an eye out for spies.

Attack on Harpers Ferry

The last three members of the raiding party arrived at the Kennedy farm on October 15. The attack on Harpers Ferry began the following evening. The raiders cut telegraph wires, took dozens of hostages, and easily captured the arsenal, which was lightly guarded.

Everything appeared to go smoothly until a train en route from Wheeling to Baltimore approached Harpers Ferry. First, a wounded night watchman warned the train conductor that the town was under attack. Next, a baggage handler—a free black man named Hayward Shepherd— emerged from the train station and attempted to alert the passengers to the danger they faced. Brown's men yelled at him to halt, then shot him to death.

A wiser leader might have ordered his men to keep the train stopped at Harpers Ferry, snatch as many weapons from the arsenal as they could, and retreat to the hills. Brown did none of these things. Instead, he let the train proceed eastward toward the town of Frederick, from where U.S. government leaders could be alerted that a rebellion was under way. Brown and his men remained at Harpers Ferry with their stacks of rifles, expecting a flood of newly free slaves to join them there. It didn't happen.

Counterattack and Capture

Word of the Harpers Ferry revolt spread through the surrounding countryside. Soon, armed white farmers and militia men converged on the town. Their rifle fire kept Brown's raiders pinned down at the armory until federal troops could arrive.

Brown spent the night of October 17 in a small brick building that served as an engine house (and later became known as "Brown's Fort").

The illustration shows U.S. Marines storming "Brown's Fort" on October 18, 1859. Commanding the Marines that day was Robert E. Lee— famous a few years later as a Confederate Army leader in the Civil War.

"John Brown's Body"

One of the best-known songs of the Civil War tells a story about John Brown. A familiar version of this song begins:

John Brown's body lies a mouldering in the grave….

Surprisingly, this song wasn't originally written to honor the famous abolitionist. The words about Brown were a joke composed at the expense of another man named John Brown, a soldier in the Massachusetts 12th Regiment. When Union soldiers from other states and regiments picked up the tune, they didn't know the whole story. They sang it as a simple way of honoring one of their heroes, the man who had struck a blow against slavery at Harpers Ferry.

Julia Ward Howe—the wife of Dr. Samuel Gridley Howe, one of John Brown's "Secret Six" backers—heard Union soldiers singing the song in 1861. She took the tune and set these words to it:

Mine eyes have seen the glory of the
coming of the Lord:
He is trampling out the vintage where the grapes
of wrath are stored;
He hath loosed the fateful lightning of
His terrible swift sword:
His truth is marching on.
Glory, glory, hallelujah!
Glory, glory, hallelujah!
Glory, glory, hallelujah!
His truth is marching on.

This version, known as "The Battle Hymn of the Republic," is still sung today.

He had only four uninjured men with him, along with 11 hostages. Also in the engine house were Watson and Oliver Brown, both dying of wounds they had received in the fighting.

By the following morning, U.S. Marines commanded by Robert E. Lee had the engine house surrounded. They called on Brown and his men to surrender. Brown refused. The Marines then stormed "Brown's Fort," beat up the old man, and took him prisoner.

A Final Verdict

Brown was accused of murder and treason. The outcome of his trial was never in doubt. It took a jury only 45 minutes to convict him. Before the court sentenced him to death, he said:

> *If it is deemed necessary that I should forfeit my life for the furtherance of the ends of justice, and mingle my blood with the blood of millions in this slave country whose rights are disregarded by wicked, cruel, and unjust enactments, I say let it be done.*

Brown's death by hanging in Charles Town on December 2, 1859, did not end the debates over the kind of man he was and what he accomplished. Was he a freedom fighter or a mass murderer?

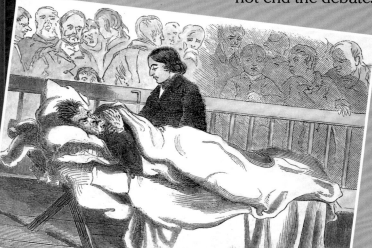

During his trial, Brown continued to suffer from wounds he had received when captured by federal troops.

Saying Goodbye

Mary Ann Day Brown last saw her husband alive on December 1, 1859, in Charles Town (now in West Virginia). They talked about her future and their daughters' schooling. The only time Brown lost control of his emotions was when his jailer said that Mary would not be allowed to stay with him overnight.

After Brown was executed on December 2, his body was delivered to Mary. She accompanied it on the train ride northward. In New York City his body was removed from its southern-made box and placed in a more suitable coffin. Church bells tolled as his body passed through New York towns on the way to North Elba. He was buried there on December 8, 1859.

Mary outlived her husband by nearly 25 years. In 1864, she traveled to California with four of her children and two grandchildren. She died in Saratoga, California, on February 29, 1884.

NEW YORK, SATURDAY, DECEMBER 17, 1859.

JOHN BROWN'S LAST INTERVIEW WITH HIS WIFE IN THE JAIL AT CHARLESTOWN, VA.

Brown's final hours captured the imagination of illustrators in the 1800s. One print (top) portrays the abolitionist embracing his wife on the day before his execution. A second print (bottom) shows him ascending the gallows moments before he was hanged.

A success or a failure? Clear-headed or insane? Disputes about Brown persisted long after the Civil War and continue to the present day.

"Did John Brown fail?" asked Frederick Douglass, a black man who had known his fellow abolitionist for more than 20 years. "John Brown began the war that ended American slavery and made this a free Republic. His zeal in the cause of my race was far greater than mine. I could live for the slave, but he could die for him."

JOHN BROWN
1800 – 1859

John Brown's grave (left) is located at the John Brown Farm and Gravesite, a National Historic Site at North Elba, New York. Near the gravestone is a statue of Brown with a young African-American boy (right), erected in 1935.

Chronology

1800 John Brown is born May 9 in Torrington, Connecticut. He is the fourth child born to Owen Brown and Ruth Mills Brown.

1805 The Brown family moves to Hudson, Ohio, where Owen Brown opens a tannery and teaches his son the same trade.

1808 Ruth Brown dies in childbirth on December 9.

1812 While traveling in Michigan, John Brown is horrified at the sight of a slave owner beating a slave boy with an iron shovel.

1820 Brown marries Dianthe Lusk on June 21.

1832 Dianthe dies August 10, three days after her seventh child is stillborn.

1833 Brown marries Mary Ann Day on June 14. They have 13 children together.

1837 A steep economic downturn brings hardship to Brown and his family. His church expels him for urging black worshipers to sit in seats that had been reserved for white people. After a white mob kills Elijah Parish Lovejoy, an anti-slavery editor in Alton, Illinois, Brown pledges to devote the rest of his life to ending slavery.

1839 Brown begins drawing up plans to lead an army to invade the South and free the slaves.

1842 After his businesses fail, a court declares Brown bankrupt.

1843 In September, disease claims the lives of four of his children.

1846 Brown opens a wool warehouse and marketing center in Springfield, Massachusetts.

1847 Meeting with the African-American abolitionist Frederick Douglass, Brown outlines in detail his plan to lead a slave revolt.

1849 Brown settles on a farm in North Elba, New York, where black people and white people live together as equals.

1850 Congress passes the Fugitive Slave Act.

1851 Brown forms the League of Gileadites to help runaway slaves defend themselves against slave catchers.

1854 Passage of the Kansas-Nebraska Act leads to violent clashes between pro-slavery and anti-slavery settlers in Kansas. Brown arrives in Kansas the following year to support the anti-slavery forces.

1856 In May, Brown and his followers murder five pro-slavery settlers at Pottawatomie Creek, Kansas. Pro-slavery Border Ruffians kill his son Frederick at Osawatomie in August.

1857 In the Dred Scott case, the U.S. Supreme Court rules that slaves are not citizens and that Congress has no power to stop the spread of slavery.

1859 On October 16, Brown and his followers seize the federal arsenal at Harpers Ferry, Virginia (now West Virginia). He is captured two days later after a battle that claims the lives of his two sons, Watson and Oliver. Convicted of treason and murder, Brown is hanged in Charles Town on December 2.

1861 The Civil War begins April 12 when Confederate forces fire on Fort Sumter in Charleston, South Carolina.

1865 With the defeat of the South in the Civil War, the 13th Amendment to the Constitution bans slavery throughout the United States.

Glossary

abolitionist Someone who calls for an end to a particular practice, especially slavery.

amendment A change made to the original Constitution; for example, the 13th Amendment abolished slavery in 1865.

arsenal A place where weapons are made and stored.

arrogant Self-important; conceited; overbearing.

assassin A killer.

bondage Slavery, or any condition that feels like it.

Border Ruffians Heavily armed pro-slavery forces who crossed the border from Missouri into Kansas Territory.

census An official count of the number of people living in a particular area.

Civil War The war fought from 1861 to 1865 between the northern and southern U.S. states. It began when the South (or Confederacy) rebelled against the Union. The war, which was won by the North, brought an end to slavery in the United States.

consecrate To dedicate; commit to a sacred purpose.

Constitution The basic law of the United States, which took effect in 1789.

convention A large meeting or conference.

dysentery An intestinal disease that causes severe diarrhea and loss of blood throughout the digestive system.

enactments Laws.

fanatic A person who holds extreme or uncompromising views.

forfeit To give up; surrender.

fugitive Someone who flees to avoid arrest, capture, or ill treatment; a runaway.

gallows A device from which criminals are hanged to death.

indignation Anger or outrage directed at something that is considered unfair or unjust.

industrious Hardworking.

League of Gileadites (pronounced "gil-ee-uh-dites") An African-American self-defense group organized by John Brown in 1851 in Springfield, Massachusetts.

legislature The branch of government that has the power to make laws; a group of people elected or chosen for that purpose.

liberate To set free.

memorial service An event or gathering to honor the memory of someone who has died.

militia A fighting force consisting of ordinary citizens rather than full-time soldiers.

mouldering Rotting; decaying.

New England In the northeastern United States, a region that includes Connecticut, Maine, Massachusetts, New Hampshire, Rhode Island, and Vermont.

Panic of 1837 A steep economic downturn in which many banks collapsed and businesses failed.

purge To get rid of something that is undesirable or unwanted; to cleanse or purify.

regiment A unit of the armed forces.

Revolutionary War Armed conflict (1775–1783) in which 13 British colonies in North America rebelled against continued rule by Great Britain; the war ended with Britain's recognition of the former colonies as the United States of America.

secluded Hidden; private; out of the way.

sue To bring a court case against someone.

tanner Someone who turns animal skins into leather.

treason The crime of knowingly aiding the enemies of a government or seeking to overthrow it.

Underground Railroad The secret network of people who helped slaves escape from the South to the North and then across the border into Canada.

War of 1812 Conflict between the United States and Great Britain; the war, which lasted until early 1815, ended with no clear winner.

Further Information

Books

Brackett, Virginia. *John Brown: Abolitionist* (Famous Figures of the Civil War Era). Chelsea House, 2001.

DeVillers, David. *The John Brown Slavery Revolt Trial (A Headline Court Case)* Enslow, 2000.

Sterngass, Jon. *John Brown* (Leaders of the Civil War Era). Chelsea House, 2009.

Tackach, James. *The Trial of John Brown, Radical Abolitionist* (Famous Trials). Lucent Books, 1998.

Videos

The American Experience: John Brown's Holy War (DVD). PBS Home Video, 2000.

Web sites

www.law.umkc.edu/faculty/projects/ftrials/johnbrown/ brownhome.html
An in-depth study of John Brown's 1859 trial, put together by Douglas O. Linder of the University of Missouri–Kansas City School of Law. Documents here include a full report of the court events and John Brown's last letters to his wife and children.

www.nps.gov/hafe
The National Park Service provides an online guide to Harpers Ferry National Historical Park. A photo slideshow offers a virtual tour of the park, which spans parts of three states: West Virginia, Maryland, and Virginia. In a series of video clips, Stephen B. Oates, an expert on John Brown, answers questions about the abolitionist leader.

www.pbs.org/wgbh/amex/brown/
Designed to supplement the PBS video on John Brown, this Web site has a timeline, maps, and special features on the people and events that figured in Brown's life.

Index

Index

About the Author

Geoffrey M. Horn has written more than four dozen books for young people and adults, along with hundreds of articles for encyclopedias and other works. He lives in southwestern Virginia, in the foothills of the Blue Ridge Mountains, with his wife, their collie, and five cats. He dedicates this book to P.A. and Dot Harman.

Printed in the USA—BG